STO ✓

Keep in
Adult N.F.
Nov. 18, 69

Sep 1
shu 1

D1213708

Libretto for the Republic of Liberia

Libretto for the
Republic of Liberia

M. B. Tolson

TWAYNE PUBLISHERS, INC.
NEW YORK

Grateful acknowledgment for the
reprinting of the *Preface* and section
TI of this poem is made to *Poetry
Magazine*.

To

Mary McLeod Bethune

PREFACE

DOUBTLESS, MR. TOLSON DOES NOT EXPECT HIS LIBRETTO TO HAVE a musical setting; or if he does, one wonders what an audience would make of it. Official celebrations in Liberia cannot differ greatly from those in Washington or Paris, where the apathy of polite inattention is usually all that an official poem deserves. One can imagine, in Washington, during the New Deal, a patriotic poem being read by the late Stephen Vincent Benèt; but not, I assume, by the late Hart Crane. That may be one difference between the literary culture of official Washington and that of Liberia: Mr. Tolson is in the direct succession from Crane. Here is something marvellous indeed. A small African republic founded by liberated slaves celebrates its centenary by getting an American Negro poet to write what, in the end, is an English Pindaric ode in a style derived from—but by no means merely imitative of—one of the most difficult modern poets.

What irony we are entitled to infer from Mr. Tolson's official appointment to this job I am not prepared to guess. I leave the question with the remark that I cannot imagine a white American poet of equal distinction being given a similar job by President Truman.

For there is a great gift for language, a profound historical sense, and a first-rate intelligence at work in this poem from first to last. On the first page I received a shock, in that region where bored scepticism awaits the new manuscript from a poet not clearly identified, when I saw Liberia invoked as

... the quicksilver sparrow that slips
The eagle's claw!

From that passage to the end I read the poem with increasing attention and admiration.

The poem is in eight sections mounting to a climax which is rhetorically effective but not, I think, quite successful as poetry. The last section begins in a six-line stanza which is controlled with considerable mastery, but the movement breaks down into Whitmanesque prose-paragraphs into which Mr. Tolson evidently felt that he could toss all the loose ends of history, objurgation, and prophecy which the set theme seemed to require of him as official poet. Nevertheless, even this part of the poem is written with great energy. I point out what I consider its defects only because the power and versatility of other parts of the poem offset them, and enjoin the critic to pay the poem the compliment of very severe scrutiny.

What influence this work will have upon Negro poetry in the United States one awaits with curiosity. For the first time, it seems to me, a Negro poet has assimilated completely the full poetic language of his time and, by implication, the language of the Anglo-American poetic tradition. I do not wish to be understood as saying that Negro poets have hitherto been incapable of this assimilation; there has been perhaps rather a resistance to it on the part of those Negroes who supposed that their peculiar genius lay in "folk" idiom or in the romantic creation of a "new" language within the English language. In these directions interesting and even distinguished work has been done, notably by Langston Hughes and Gwendolyn Brooks. But there are two disadvantages to this approach: first, the "folk" and "new" languages are not very different from those that White poets can write; secondly, the distinguishing Negro quality is not in the language but in the subject-matter, which is usually the plight of the Negro segregated in a White culture. The plight is real and often tragic; but I cannot think that, *from the literary point of view,* the tragic aggressiveness of the modern Negro poet offers wider poetic possibilities than the resigned pathos of Paul Laurence Dunbar, who was only a "White" *poète manqué.* Both attitudes have limited the Negro poet to a provincial mediocrity in which one's feelings about one's difficulties become more important than poetry itself.

It seems to me only common sense to assume that the main thing is the poetry, if one is a poet, whatever one's color may be. I think that Mr. Tolson has assumed this; and the assumption, I gather, has made him not less but more intensely *Negro* in his apprehension of the world than any of his contemporaries, or any that I have read. But by becoming more intensely Negro he seems to me to dismiss the entire problem, so far as poetry is concerned, by putting it in its properly subordinate place. In the end I found that I was reading *Libretto for the Republic of Liberia* not because Mr. Tolson is a Negro but because he is a poet, not because the poem has a "Negro subject" but because it is about the world of all men. And this subject is not merely asserted; it is embodied in a rich and complex language, and realized in terms of the poetic imagination.

ALLEN TATE

Libretto for the Republic of Liberia

DO

Liberia?
No micro-footnote in a bunioned book
Homed by a pedant
With a gelded look:
You are
The ladder of survival dawn men saw
In the quicksilver sparrow that slips
The eagle's claw!

Liberia?
No side-show barker's bio-accident,   10
No corpse of a soul's errand
To the Dark Continent:
You are
The lightning rod of Europe, Canaan's key,
The rope across the abyss,
Mehr licht for the Africa-To-Be!

Liberia?
No haply black man's X
Fixed to a Magna Charta without a magic-square
By Helon's leprous hand, to haunt and vex: 20
You are
The Orient of Colors everywhere,
The oasis of Tahoua, the salt bar of Harrar,
To trekkers in saharas, in sierras, with Despair!

Liberia?
No oil-boiled Barabas,
No Darwin's bulldog for ermined flesh,
No braggart Lamech, no bema's Ananias:
You are
Libertas flayed and naked by the road   30
To Jericho, for a people's five score years
Of bones for manna, for balm an alien goad!

Liberia?
No pimple on the chin of Africa,
No brass-lipped cicerone of Big Top democracy,
No lamb to tame a lion with a baa:
You are
Black Lazarus risen from the White Man's grave,
Without a road to Downing Street,
Without a hemidemisemiquaver in an Oxford stave!   40

Liberia?
No Cobra Pirate of the Question Mark,
No caricature with a mimic flag
And golden joys to fat the shark:
You are
American genius uncrowned in Europe's charnel-house.
Leave fleshpots for the dogs and apes; for Man
The books whose head is golden espouse!

Liberia?
No waste land yet, nor yet a destooled elite,   50
No merry-andrew, an Ed-dehebi at heart,
With St. Paul's root and Breughel's cheat:
You are
The iron nerve of lame and halt and blind,
Liberia and not Liberia,
A moment of the conscience of mankind!

The Good Gray Bard in Timbuktu chanted:
"Brow tron lo — eta ne a ne won oh gike!"

Before Liberia was, Songhai was: before
America set the raw foundling on Africa's   60
Doorstep, before the Genoese diced west,
Burnt warriors and watermen of Songhai
Tore into *bizarreries* the uniforms of Portugal
And sewed an imperial quilt of tribes.

In Milan and Mecca, in Balkh and Bombay,
Sea lawyers in the eyeservice of sea kings
Mixed liquors with hyperboles to cure deafness.
Europe bartered Africa crucifixes for red ivory,
Gewgaws for black pearls, *pierres d'aigris* for green gold:
Soon the rivers and roads became clog almanacs!   70

The Good Gray Bard in Timbuktu chanted:
"Wanawake wanazaa ovyo! Kazi yenu wazungu!"

Black Askia's fetish was his people's health:
The world his world, he gave the Bengal light
Of Books the Inn of Court in Songhai. *Beba mzigo!*
The law of empathy set the market price,
Scaled the word and deed: the gravel-blind saw
Deserts give up the ghost to green pastures!

Solomon in all his glory had no Oxford,
Alfred the Great no University of Sankoré: 80
Footloose professors, chimney sweeps of the skull,
From Europe and Asia; youths, souls in one skin,
Under white scholars like El-Akit, under
Black humanists like Bagayogo. *Karibu wee!*

The Good Gray Bard in Timbuktu chanted:
"Europe is an empty python in hiding grass!"

Lia! Lia! The river Wagadu, the river Bagana,
Became dusty metaphors where white ants ate canoes,
And the locust Portuguese raped the maiden crops,
And the sirocco Spaniard razed the city-states,   90
And the leopard Saracen bolted his scimitar into
The jugular vein of Timbuktu. *Dieu seul est grand!*

And now the hyenas whine among the barren bones
Of the seventeen sun sultans of Songhai,
And hooded cobras, hoodless mambas, hiss
In the gold caverns of Falémé and Bambuk,
And puff adders, hook scorpions, whisper
In the weedy corridors of Sankoré. *Lia! Lia!*

The Good Gray Bard chants no longer in Timbuktu:
"The maggots fat on yeas and nays of nut empires!"   100

MI

Before the bells of Yankee capital
Tolled for the feudal glory of the South
And Frederick Douglass's Vesuvian mouth
Erupted amens crushing Copperheads,

Old Robert Finley, Jehovah's Damasias,
Swooped into Pennsylvania Avenue
To pinion Henry Clay, the shuttlecock,
And Bushrod Washington, whose family name

Dwarfed signatures of blood: his magnet Yea
Drew Lawyer Key, the hymnist primed to match   110
A frigate's guns, and Bishop Meade, God's purse,
And Doctor Torrey, the People's clock: they eagled

The gospel for the wren Republic in
Supreme Court chambers. That decision's cash
And credit bought a balm for conscience, verved
Black Pilgrim Fathers to Cape Mesurado,

Where sun and fever, brute and vulture, spelled
The idioms of their faith in whited bones.
No linguist of the Braille of prophecy ventured:
The rubber from Liberia shall arm   120

Free peoples and her airport hinterlands
Let loose the winging grapes of wrath upon
The Desert Fox's cocained nietzscheans
A goosestep from the Gateway of the East!

FA

A fabulous mosaic log,
        the Bola boa lies
            gorged to the hinges of his jaws,
            eyeless, yet with eyes . . .

in the interlude of peace.

The beaked and pouched assassin sags   130
    on to his corsair rock,
    and from his talons swim the blood-
    red feathers of a cock . . .

in the interlude of peace.

The tawny typhoon striped with black
    torpors in grasses tan:
    a doomsday cross, his paws uprear
    the leveled skull of a man . . .

in the interlude of peace

SOL

White Pilgrims, turn your trumpets west!   140
Black Pilgrims, *shule, agrah,* nor tread
The Skull of another's stairs!

This is the horned American
Dilemma: yet, this too, O Christ,
This too, O Christ, will pass!

The brig *Elizabeth* flaunts her stern
At auction blocks with the eyes of Cain
And down-the-river sjamboks.

This is the Middle Passage: here
Gehenna hatchways vomit up   150
The debits of pounds of flesh.

This is the Middle Passage: here
The sharks wax fattest and the stench
Goads God to hold His nose!

Elijah Johnson, his *Tygers heart*
In the whale's belly, flenses midnight:
"How long? How long? How long?"

A dark age later the answer dawns
When whitecap pythons thrash upon
The molar teeth of reefs   160

And hallelujahs quake the brig
From keel to crow's-nest and tomtoms gibber
In cosmic *deepi-talki.*

Elijah feels the Forty Nights'
Octopus reach up to drag his mind
Into man's genesis.

He hears the skulls plowed under cry:
"*Griots,* the quick owe the quick and dead.
A man owes man to man!"

"*Seule de tous les continents,*" the parrots   170
chatter, "*l'Afrique n'a pas d'histoire!*"
Mon petit doigt me l'a dit:

"Africa is a rubber ball;
the harder you dash it to the ground,
the higher it will rise.

"A lie betrays its mother tongue.
The Eye said, 'Ear, the Belly is
the foremost of the gods.'

"Fear makes a gnarl a cobra's head.
One finger cannot kill a louse.   180
The seed waits for the lily.

"No fence's legs are long enough.
The lackey licks the guinea's boot
till holes wear in the tongue.

"A camel on its knees solicits
the ass's load. Potbellies cook
no meals for empty maws.

"When skins are dry the flies go home.
Repentance is a peacock's tail.
The cock is yolk and feed.   190

"Three steps put man one step ahead.
The rich man's weights are not the poor
man's scales. To each his coole.

"A stinkbug should not peddle perfume.
The tide that ebbs will flow again.
A louse that bites is in

"the inner shirt. An open door
sees both inside and out. The saw
that severs the topmost limb

"comes from the ground. God saves the black   200
man's soul but not his buttocks from
the white man's lash. The mouse

"as artist paints a mouse that chases
a cat. The diplomat's lie is fat
at home and lean abroad.

"It is the grass that suffers when
two elephants fight. The white man solves
between white sheets his black

"problem. Where would the rich cream be
without skim milk? The eye can cross   210
the river in a flood.

"Law is a rotten tree; black man, rest
thy weight elsewhere, or like the goat
outrun the white man's stink!"

Elijah broods: "The fevers hoed
Us under at Sherbro. Leopard saints
Puked us from Bushrod Beach

"To Providence Island, where John Mill,
The mulatto trader, fended off
The odds that bait the hook.   220

"The foxes have holes, the birds have nests,
And I have found a place to lay
My head, Lord of Farewells!"

And every ark awaits its raven,
Its vesper dove with an olive-leaf,
Its rainbow over Ararat.

LA

Glaciers had shouldered down
The cis-Saharan snows,
Shoved antelope and lion
Past *Uaz-Oîriet* floes.   230

Leopard, elephant, ape,
Rhinoceros and giraffe
Jostled in odysseys
To Africa: siamang laugh

And curse impaled the frost
As Northmen brandished paws
And shambled Europe-ward,
Gnashing Cerberean jaws.

After *netami lennowak,*
A white man spined with dreams   240
Came to cudgel parrot scholars
And slay philistine schemes.

"The lion's teeth, the eagle's
Talons, shall break!" declared
Prophet Jehudi Ashmun,
Christening the bones that dared.

When the black bat's ultima smote
His mate in the yoke, he felt
The seven swords' *pis aller*
Twist in his heart at the hilt.   250

He said: "My Negro kinsmen,
America is my mother,
Liberia is my wife,
And Africa my brother."

TI

O Calendar of the Century,
red-letter the Republic's birth!
O Hallelujah,
oh, let no *Miserere*
venom the spinal cord of Afric earth!
Selah!   260

"Ecce homo!"
the blind men cowled in azure rant
before the Capitol,
between the Whale and Elephant,
where no longer stands Diogenes' hearse
readied for the ebony mendicant,
nor weeping widow Europe with her hands
making the multitudinous seas incarnadine
or earth's *massebôth* worse:
O Great White World, thou boy of tears, omega hounds   270
lap up the alpha laugh and *du-haut-en-bas* curse.
Selah!

O Africa, Mother of Science
. . . *lachen mit yastchekes* . . .
What dread hand,
to make tripartite one august event,
sundered Gondwanaland?
What dread grasp crushed your biceps and
back upon the rack
chaos of chance and change   280
fouled in Malebolgean isolation?
What dread *elboga* shoved your soul
into the *tribulum* of retardation?
melamin or melanin dies to the world and dies:
Rome casketed herself in Homeric hymns.
Man's culture in barb and Arab lies:
The Jordan flows into the Tiber,
the Yangtze into the Thames,
the Ganges into the Mississippi, the Niger
into the Seine.   290
Judge of the Nations, spare us: yet,
fool latins, alumni of one school,
on Clochan-na-n'all, say *Phew*
. . . *Lest we forget! Lest we forget!* . . .
to dusky peers of Roman, Greek, and Jew.
Selah!

Elders of Agâ's House, keening
at the Eagles' feast, cringing
before the Red Slayer, shrinking
from the blood on Hubris' pall—   300
carked by cracks of myriad curbs,
hitherto, against the Wailing Wall
of Ch'in, the blind men cried:
All cultures crawl
walk hard
fall,
flout
under classes under
Lout,
enmesh in ethos, in *masôreth,* the poet's flesh,   310
intone the Mass of the class as the requiem of the mass,
serve *adola mentis* till the crack of will,
castle divorcee Art in a blue-blood moat,
read the flesh of grass
into bulls and bears,
let Brahmin pens kill
Everyman the Goat,
write Culture's epitaph in *Notes* upstairs.
O *Cordon Sanitaire,*
thy brain's tapeworm, extract, thy eyeball's mote!   320
Selah!

Between pavilions
small and great
sentineled from capital to stylobate
by crossbow, harquebus, cannon, or Pegasus' bomb
. . . *and none went in and none went out* . . .
hitherto the State,
in spite of Sicilian Vespers, stout
from slave, feudal, bourgeois, or soviet grout,
has hung its curtain — scrim, foulard, pongee,   330
silk, lace, or iron — helled in by Sancho's fears
of the bitter hug of the Great Fear, Not-To-Be —
oscuro Luzbel,
with no bowels of mercy,
in the starlight
de las canteras sin auroras.
Behind the curtain, aeon after aeon,
he who doubts the white book's colophon
is Truth's, if not Laodicean, wears
the black flower T of doomed Laocoön.   340
Before hammer and sickle or swastika, two
worlds existed: the Many, the Few.
They sat at Delos', at Vienna's, at Yalta's, ado:
Macbeth, without three rings, as host
to Banquo's ghost.
Selah!

Like some gray ghoul from Alcatraz,
old Profit, the bald rake *paseq*, wipes the bar,
polishes the goblet vanity,
leers at the tigress Avarice   350
as
she harlots roués from afar:
swallowtails unsaved by loincloths,
famed enterprises prophesying war,
hearts of rags (*Hanorish tharah sharinas*) souls of chalk,
laureates with sugary grace in zinc buckets of verse,
myths rattled by the blueprint's talk,
ists potted and pitted by a feast,
Red Ruin's skeleton horsemen, four abreast
. . . galloping . . .   360
Marx, the exalter, would not know his East
. . . galloping . . .
nor Christ, the Leveler, His West.
Selah!

O Age of Tartuffe
. . . *a lighthouse with no light atop* . . .
O Age, *pesiq*, O Age,
kinks internal and global stinks
fog the bitter black estates of Buzzard and Og.
A Dog, I'd rather be, o sage, a Monkey or a Hog.   370
O Peoples of the Brinks,
come with the hawk's resolve,
the skeptic's optic nerve, the prophet's *tele* verve
and Oedipus' guess, to solve
the riddle of
the Red Enigma and the White Sphinx.
Selah!

O East . . . *el grito de Dolores* . . . O West,
 pacts, disemboweled, crawl off to die;
 white books, *fiers instants promis à la faux*,   380
 in sick bay choke on mulligan truth and lie;
 the knife of Rousseau hacks the anatomy
    of the fowl necessity;
  dead eyes accuse red Desfourneau,
whose sit-down strike gives High-Heels vertigo;
  the wind blows through the keyhole
 and the fettered pull down the shades;
 while *il santo* and *pero* hone phillipics,
Realpolitik explodes the hand grenades
    faits accomplis   390
   in the peace of parades;
 caught in the blizzard *divide et impera,*
  the little gray cattle cower
  before the Siamese wolves,
   pomp and power;
 Esperanto trips the heels of Greek;
in brain-sick lands, the pearls too rich for swine
 the claws of the anonymous seek;
 the case Caesarean, Lethean brew
 nor instruments obstetrical at hand,   400
the midwife of the old disenwombs the new.
    Selah!

  The *Höhere* of Gaea's children
is beyond the *dérèglement de tous les sens,* is beyond
 gold fished from cesspools, the *galerie des rois,*
 the seeking of cows, *apartheid,* Sisyphus' despond,
the Ilande intire of itselfe with *die Schweine* in mud,
 the potter's wheel that stocks the potter's field,
Kchesinskaja's balcony with epitaphs in blood,
 deeds hostile all, O Caton, to hostile eyes,   410
 the breaking of foreheads against the walls,
 gazing at navels, thinking with thighs

   . . .

The *Höhere* of God's stepchildren
is beyond the sabotaged world, is beyond
das Diktat der Menschenverachtung,
la muerte sobre el esqueleto de la nada,
the pelican's breast rent red to feed the young,
summer's third-class ticket, the *Revue des morts,*
the skulls trepanned to hold ideas plucked from dung,
Dives' crumbs in the church of the unchurched,   420
absurd life shaking its ass's ears among
the colors of vowels and Harrar blacks
with Nessus shirts from Europe on their backs

                    . . .

The *Höhere* of X's children
is beyond Heralds' College, the *filets d'Arachné,* is beyond
maggot democracy, the *Mal éternel,* the Bells of Ys,
the doddering old brigades with aorist medicines of poetry,
the *Orizaba* with its Bridge of Sighs,
the *oasis d'horreur dans un déserte d'ennui,*
the girasol rocks of Secunderabad,   430
Yofan's studio and *Shkola Nenavisti,*
the *otototoi* — in Crimson Tapestries — of the *hoi polloi,*
Euboean defeats
in the Sausage Makers' bout
the fool himself himself finds out
and in the cosmos of his chaos
repeats.
Selah!

The *Höhere* of one's pores *En Masse*
. . . Christians, Jews, *ta ethne* . . .   440
          makes as apishly
brazen as the brag and brabble of brass
          the flea's fiddling
          on the popinjay,
          the pollack's pout
          in the net's hurray,
          the jerboa's feat
        in the fawn and the flout
              of
            Quai d'Orsay,   450
            White House,
            Kremlin,
        Downing Street.
Again black Aethiop reaches at the sun, O Greek.
Things-as-they-are-for-us, *nullius in verba,*
              speak!
          O East, O West,
        on tenotomy bent,
          Chang's tissue is
          Eng's ligament!   460
            Selah!

Between Yesterday's wars
now hot now cold
the grief-in-grain of Man
dripping dripping dripping
from the Cross of Iron
dripping
drew jet vampires
of the Skull;
Between Yesterday's wills of Tanaka, between   470
golden goblet and truckling trull
and the ires
of rivers red with the reflexes of fires,
the ferris wheel
of race, of caste, of class
dumped and alped cadavers till the ground
fogged the Pleiades with Gila rot: Today the mass,
the Beast with a Maginot Line in its Brain,
the staircase Avengers of base alloy,
the *vile canaille* — *Gorii!* — the *Bastard-rasse*,   480
the *uomo qualyque*, the *hoi barbaroi*,
the *raya* in the *Oeil de Boeuf*,
the *vsechelovek*, the *descamisados*, the *hoi polloi*,
the Raw from the Coliseum of the Cooked,
Il Duce's Whore, Vardaman's Hound —
unparadised nobodies with maps of Nowhere
ride the merry-go-round!
Selah!

a *pelageya* in *as seccas* the old she-fox today
eyes dead letters mouth a hole in a privy   490
   taschunt a corpse's in a mud-walled troy of *jagunços*
   (*naze naze desu ka servant de dakar*) (*el grito de yara*)
     cackles among the garbage cans of mummy truths
     o frontier saints bring out your dead

the aria of the old *sookin sin* breaks my shoulders
lasciatemi morire o africa (*maneno matupu*)
   the fat of fame didn't outlast a night in hog's wash
   nor geneva's church nor the savage's ten pounds
     for stratford's poor (bles be ye man for jesvs sake)
     here one singeth *per me si va nella città dolente*   500

below the triumvirate flag & tongue & mammon
while *blut und boden* play the anthemn *iron masters gold*
   ruble shilling franc yen lira baht and dime
   brass-knuckled (*la légalité nous tue*) and iron-toed
     wage armageddon in the temple of *dieu et l'état*
     o earl of queensberry o last christian on the cross

vexilla regis prodeunt inferni what is man f.r.a.i. *tò tí*
(a professor of metaphysicotheologicocosmonigology
   a tooth puller a pataphysicist in a cloaca of error
   a belly's wolf a skull's tabernacle a #13 with stars   510
     a muses' darling a busie bee *de sac et de corde*
     a neighbor's bed-shaker a walking hospital on the walk)

lincoln walks the midnight epoch of the ant-hill
and barbaric yawps shatter the shoulder-knots of white peace
   jai hind (dawn comes up like thunder) *pakinstan zindabad*
   britannia rules the waves *my pokazhem meeru*
      the world is my parish *muhammad rasulu 'llah*
      hara ga hette iru oh yeah *higashi no kazeame*

naïfs pray for a guido's scale of good and evil to match
worldmusic's sol-fa syllables (*o do de do de do de*)   520
   worldmathematics' arabic and roman figures
   worldscience's greek and latin symbols
      the letter killeth five hundred global tongues
      before esperanto garrotes voläpuk *vanitas vanitatum*

o majesty-dwarf'd brothers *en un solo espasmo sexual*
ye have mock'd the golden rules of eleven sons of god
   smitten to rubble *ein feste burg* for a few acres of snow
   buried the open sesame *satya bol gat hai* among dry bones
      wasted the balm *assalamu aleykum* on lice and maggots
      snarled the long spoon for the scaly horror   530

pin-pricks precede blitzkriegs *mala' oun el yom yomek*
idiots carol happy dashes in st. innocent's little acre
   of rags and bones without brasses black and red
   booby mouths looted of the irritating parenthesis
      patrol skulls unhonored by a cromwell's pike
      snaggleteeth glutted *in sudori vultus alieni*

o sweet chariot these aesop's flies without mirth
these *oh-mono* without music in greed's akeldama
   are one with the great auk of the north star
   mouldy rolls of noah's ark and wall street   540
      nuclei fed to demogorgon's mill
      alms for oblivion raindrops minus h_2o

o's without figures on ice the sun licks
pebbles let fall in the race of a night sea
    jockeyed by beaufort no. 12
      iotas of the *yod* of god in a rolls royce
        the seven trumpets of today's baby boys summon peace
        and the walls come tumblin' down (christ sleeps)

and no mourners go crying *dam-bid-dam*
about the ex-streets of scarlet letters   550
    only the souls of hyenas whining *teneo te africa*
    only the blind men gibbering *mboagan* in greek
      against sodom's pillars of salt
      below the mountain of rodinsmashedstatues *aleppe*

. . . .

Tomorrow . . . O . . . Tomorrow,
Where is the glory of the *mestizo* Pharaoh?
The Mahdi's tomb of the foul deed?
Black Clitus of the fatal verse and Hamlet's arras?
The cesspool of the reef of gold?
Der Schwarze Teufel, Napoleon's savior?   560
The Black Virgin of Creation's Hell Hole?
Tomorrow . . . O . . . Tomorrow,
Where is Jugurtha the dark Iago?
The witches' Sabbath of sleeping sickness?
The *Nye ke mi* eyeless in the River of Blood?
The Tagus that imitates the Congo?
The *Mein Kampf* of *kitab al sudan wa'lbidan?*
The black albatross about the white man's neck?
O Tomorrow,
Where is the graven image *pehleh* of *Nash Barin?*   570
Their white age of their finest black hour?
The forged minute book of ebony Hirsch?
The chattel whose Rock vies with the Rime of the upstart Crow?
Ppt. knows.

S 1446063

. . . .

The Futurafrique, the *chef d'oeuvre* of Liberian
    Motors slips through the traffic
    swirl of axial Parsifal-Feirefiz
    Square, slithers past the golden
    statues of the half-brothers as
    brothers, with *cest prace* . . .   580
The Futurafrique, the accent on youth and speed
    and beauty, escalades the Mount
    Sinai of Tubman University, the
    vistas of which bloom with co-
    eds from seven times seven lands . . .
The Futurafrique, windows periscopic, idles past
    the entrance to the 70A subway
    station, volplanes into the aria
    of Swynnerton Avenue, zooms
    by the Zorzor Monument, zigzags   590
    between the factory hierarchies,
    rockets upcountry and backcoun-
    try, arcs the ad-libbing soapy
    blue harbor crossroads of Wal-
    dorf Astorias at anchor, atom-
    fueled and burnished in ports
    of the six seagirt worlds . . .
The Futurafrique strokes the thigh of Mount Bar-
    clay and skis toward the Good-
    lowe Straightaway, whose colo-   600
    ratura sunset is the alpenglow
    of cultures in the Shovelhead Era
    of the Common Man . . .
The Futurafrique glitters past bronze Chomolungma, odic
    memorial to Matilda Newport—
    on and on and on, outracing the
    supercoach of the Momolu Bu-
    kere Black-Hound winging along
    the seven-lane Equatorial High-
    way toward Khopirû . . .   610

The Futurafrique, flight-furbished ebony astride
velvet-paved miles, vies with the
sunflower magnificence of the
Oriens, challenges the snow-lily
diadem of the Europa . . .
The Futurafrique, with but a scintilla of its Niagara
power, slices Laubach Park,
eclipses the Silver Age Gibbet
of Shikata-gai-nai, beyond the
ars of Phidias; on and on, herds   620
only blears of rotor masts roulet-
ting, estates only rococo decks
and sails swirling, the Futurafrique, the Oriens, the Auster,
the Americus, the Europa, rend
space, gut time, arrowing past
tiering Nidaba, glissading side
by side, into the cosmopolis of
Höhere — the bygone habitat of
mumbo jumbo and blue tongue,   630
of sasswood-bark jury and tsetse
fly, aeons and aeons before the
Unhappie Wight of the Question Mark crossed the Al Sirat!

The United Nations Limited volts over the unten-
anted, untitled grave of Black
Simoom, the red Chaka of *ruse
de guerre,* the Cheops of pyra-
mids with the skulls of Pygmy
and Britisher, Boer and Arab . . .   640

The United Nations Limited careers across Seretse
        Khama's Bechuanaland, yester-
        day and yesterday and yester-
        day after the body of Living-
        stone knelled its trek in dry salt
        from Lake Bangeula to the sab-
        bath of Westminster Abbey . . .
The United Nations Limited horseshoe-curves Stan-
        ley Falls, sheens the surrealistic
        harlotry of the mirage-veiled   650
        Sahara, quakes the dinosaurian
        teeth bolted in the jaws of Ti-
        besti, zoom-zooms through the
        Ptolemaic Subterane like a silver
        sirocco . . .
The United Nations Limited, stream-phrased and air-
        chamoised and sponge-cush-
        ioned, telescopes the polyge-
        netic metropolises polychro-
        matic between Casablanco and   660
        Mafeking, Freetown and Addis
        Ababa!

The Bula Matadi, diesel-engined, fourfold-decked,
        swan-sleek, glides like an ice-
        ballet skater out of the Bight of
        Benin, the lily lyricism of whose
        ivory and gold figurines larked
        space oneness on the shelf ice
        of avant-garde Art . . .
The Bula Matadi swivels past isled Ribat, where, in   670
        a leaden age's iliads, the Black
        Messiah and his Black Puritans,
        exsected by Sodoms and Go-
        morrahs, daunted doxy doubts
        with skeletons of dharna . . .

The Bula Matadi skirrs up the Niger, with her Khufu
        cargo from Tel Aviv and Hiro-
        shima, Peiping and San Salva-
        dor, Monrovia and Picayune!

Le Premier des Noirs, of Pan-African Airways, whirs   680
        beyond the copper cordilleran
        climaxes of glass skyscrapers on
        pavonine Cape Mesurado . . .
Le Premier des Noirs meteors beyond the Great White
        Way of Kpandemai, aglitter
        with the ebony *beau monde* . . .
Le Premier des Noirs waltzes across Lake Chad, curv-
        ets above the Fifth Cataract,
        wantons with the friar stars of
        the Marra Mountains, eagles its   690
        steeple-nosed prow toward the
        Very Black and the iron cur-
        tainless Kremlin!

The Parliament of African Peoples plants the winged
        lex scripta of its New Order on
        Roberts Avenue, in Bunker Hill,
        Liberia . . .
The Parliament of African Peoples pinnacles *Novus
        Homo* in the Ashmun Interna-
        tional House, where, free and   700
        joyful again, all mankind unites,
        without heralds of earth and
        water . . .
The Parliament of African Peoples churns with magic
        potions, monsoon spirits, zonal
        oscillations, kinetic credenda,
        apocalyptic projects — shudder-
        ing at its own depth, shudder-
        ing as if Shakespeare terrified
        Shakespeare . . .   710

The Parliament of African Peoples, chains riven in
an age luminous with alpha ray
ideas, rives the cycle of years
lean and fat, poises the scales
of Head and Hand, gives Science dominion over Why and
Art over How, bids Man cross
the bridge of Bifrost and drink
draughts of rases from verved
and loined apes of God with   720
leaves of grass and great audi-
ences . . .
The Parliament of African Peoples, After the Deluge,
wipes out the zymotic zombi
cult of God's wounds, exscinds
the fetid fetish Zu'lkadah, bans
the genocidal *Siyáfa,* enroots
the Kiowa anthemn *Geh Tai
Gea* . . .
The Parliament of African Peoples pedestals a new   730
golden calendar of Höhere and
quickens the death-in-life of the
unparadised with the olive al-
penstocks of the Violent Men . . .
The Parliament of African Peoples decrees the Zu'l-
hijyah of Everyman and eter-
nizes *Afrika sikeléľ iAfrika* . . .

The Parliament of African Peoples hormones the Iscariot-
cuckolded Four Freedoms, up-
holsters warehoused *unto each*   740
according as any one has need,
keystones italics ushered in by
epee Pros and Cons Incorrup-
tible, banishes cicerones of the
witch hunt under the aegis of
Flag and Cross, while the tiered
galleries and television continents hosanna the Black Jews
from the cis-Danakil Desert,
the Ashantis from the Great   750
Sierra Nile, the Hottentots from
Bushland, the Mpongwes from
the Cameroon Peoples' Republic, the Pygmies from the United
States of Outer Ubangi . . .
The Parliament of African Peoples signets forever
the *Recessional of Europe* and
trumpets the abolition of itself:
and no nation uses *Felis leo* or
Aquila heliaca as the emblem of   760
blut und boden; and the hyenas
whine no more among the barren bones of the seventeen sun-
set sultans of Songhai; and the
deserts that gave up the ghost
to green pastures chant in the
ears and teeth of the Dog, in
the Rosh Hashana of the Afric
calends: *"Honi soit qui mal y
pense!"*   770

NOTES

7. Cf. Dryden, *All for Love*, II, i:
> ". . . upon my eagle's wings
> I bore this wren, till I was tired of soaring,
> and now he mounts above me."

11. Cf. Raleigh, *The Soul's Errand.*

15. V. Nietzsche, *Thus Spake Zarathustra.*

18. Cf. Shakespeare, *Othello*, III, iii:
> "Haply, for I am black . . ."

19. *Magic-square:* a symbol of equality. The diagram consists of a number of small squares each containing a number. The numbers are so arranged that the sum of those in each of the various rows is the same. Cf. Thomson, *The City of Dreadful Night*, XXI, 1061.

20. Cf. Willis, *The Leper.*

30. The motto of Liberia: "The love of liberty brought us here."

32. Cf. Carlyle: "God has put into every white man's hand a whip to flog a black man."

38. Cf. the tavern scenes in Boulton's comic opera, *The Sailor's Farewell.*

42. *Cobra Pirate.*V. Hardy, *Les Grands Etapes de l'Histoire du Maroc*, 50-54. *The Question Mark.* The shape of the map of Africa dramatizes two schools of thought among native African scholars. To the Christian educator, Dr. James E. Kwegyir Aggrey, it is a moral interrogation point that challenges the white world. According to Dr. Nnamdi Azikiwe, the leader of the nationalistic movement on the West Coast, foreigners consider it "a ham-bone designed by destiny for the carving-knife of European imperialism." I have found very fruitful the suggestions and criticisms of Professor Diana Pierson, the Liberian, and Dr. Akiki Nyabongo, the Ugandian. I now know that the Question Mark is rough water between Scylla and Charybdis.

43. Cf. Bismarck: "They [Negroes] appear to me to be a caricature of the white man."

44. Cf. Shakespeare, *Henry IV*, III, i:
> "A foutra for the world and worldlings base!
> I speak of Africa and golden joys."

46. Cf. Emerson: "While European genius is symbolized by some majestic Corinne crowned in the capitol at Rome, American genius finds its true type in the poor negro soldier lying in the

trenches by the Potomac with his spelling book in one hand and his musket in the other." V. Maran, *Batouala*, 9: "Civilization, civilization, pride of the Europeans and charnel-house of innocents, Rabindranath Tagore, the Hindu poet, once, at Tokio, told what you are! You have built your kingdom on corpses."

48. *The books whose head is golden.* Cf. Rossetti, *Mary's Girlhood.*

50. *Destooled.* On the Gold Coast the "Stool" is the symbol of the soul of the nation, its Magna Charta. In 1900, Sir Frederick Hodgson, Governor of the Gold Coast, demanded that the Ashantis surrender their "Stool." They immediately declared war. "Destooling" is a veto exercised by the sovereign people over unpopular rulers.

51. *Ed-dehebi:* "The Master of Gold." He was the conqueror of Songhai, with its fabulous gold mines.

54. *The iron nerve.* Cf. Tennyson, *Ode on the Death of the Duke of Wellington.*

56. V. the address of Anatole France at the bier of Emile Zola.

57. Cf. *A Memoir of Tennyson,* Vol. I, 46, the letter of Arthur Hallam to William Gladstone on the Timbuktu prize poem: "I consider Tennyson as promising fair to be the greatest poet of our generation, perhaps of our century." V. Delafosse, *Les Noirs de L'Afrique.* The Schomburg Collection, in Harlem, contains many rare items on the civilization at Timbuktu. Dr. Lorenzo Turner's *Africanism in the Gullah Dialects,* by tracing West Coast derivatives to their Arabic and Moslem and Portuguese cultural roots, has revealed the catholicity and sophistication of African antiquity and exploded the theory of the Old English origin of the Gullah dialects.

58. I am informed that variations of this *eironeia* or mockery may be found in scores of African languages. It means here: "The world is too large—that's why we do not hear everything." Cf. Pliny, *Historia Naturalis,* II: "There is always something new from Africa." Also Swift:

> "So geographers, in Afric maps,
> With savage pictures fill their gaps . . ."

69. *Black pearls.* V. Shakespeare, *Two Gentlemen of Verona,* V, i. Also *Othello,* II, i:

> "Well prais'd! How if she be black and witty?"

Mr. J. A. Rogers treats the subject and time and place adequately in *Sex and Race.*

72. *Wanawake wanazaa ovyo:* "The women keep having children right and left." *Kazi yenu wazungu:* "It's the work of you white men."

75. *Beba mzigo:* "Lift the loads." This repetend is tacked on *ex tempore* to ballads growing out of a diversity of physical and spiritual experiences.

80. V. Du Bois, *The World and Africa,* a book to which I am deeply indebted for facts.

81. The nomadic pedagogues gathered at Timbuktu are not to be confused with the *vagantes* of the *Carmina Burana.*

82. *Souls in one skin.* V. Firdousi, *The Dream of Dakiki,* I, A.

84. *Karibu wee.* Among primitives hospitality is a thing poetic— and apostolic. *Jogoo linawika: Karibu wee.* "The rooster crows: Welcome!" *Mbuzi wanalia: Karibu wee.* "The goats bleat: Welcome."

87. *Lia.* The word means "weep" and seems to follow the patterns of "*otototoi*" in the Aeschylean chorus.

92. *Dieu seul est grand.* These first words of Massillon's exordium, delivered at the magnificent funeral of Louis XIV, brought the congregation to its feet in the cathedral. For an account of the destruction of Timbuktu, see the *Tarikh el-Fettach.* The *askia* Issahak, in a vain attempt to stop the Spanish renegades at Tondibi, used cows as Darius had used elephants against the Macedonian phalanx.

100. *Nut empires.* Cf. Sagittarius, *New Statesman and Nation,* May 1, 1948, the poem entitled "Pea-Nuts":
    "The sun of Empire will not set
    While Empire nuts abound."

122. The airfields of Liberia sent 17,0000 bombers a month against Rommel's *Afrika Korps.*

141. *Shule, agrah:* "Move, my heart." Cf. Sharp, *Shule, Shule, Shule, Agrah.* It is a refrain from old Gaelic ballads.

142. *Skull: "gulgoleth,"* a place of torment and martyrdom. *Another's stairs.* Cf. Rossetti, *Dante at Verona,* the epigraph from *Paradiso,* XVII:
    "Yea, thou shalt learn how salt his food who fares
    Upon another's bread—how steep his path
    Who treadeth up and down another's stairs."

143. V. Myrdal, *An American Dilemma.* Cf. Aptheker, *The Negro People in America.* Also Cox, *Race, Caste and Class.*

147. *Auction blocks.* Cf. Rolfe, *Diary, 1619:* "About the last of August came a Dutch man of warre that sold us twenty negars." Also Field, *Freedom Is More than a Word:* "And the Negroes have been in this country longer, on the average, than their white neighbors; they first came to this country on a ship called the 'Jesus' one year before the 'Mayflower' . . ." *With the eyes of Cain.* Cf. Watson, *The World in Armor.*

148. Cf. John Davis, *Travels,* the chapter on a slave hanging alive on a gibbet in South Carolina: ". . . the negur lolled out his tongue, his eyes starting from their sockets, and for three long days his only cry was Water! Water! Water!" *Sjamboks.* Cf. Padmore, *Africa:* "The Africans are housed like cattle in a compound . . . they are guarded by foremen armed with the sjambok, a hide whip—the symbol of South African civilization."

155. *Tygers heart:* Greene's allusion to "the onely Shake-scene."

163. Cf. LaVarre: "My black companions had two languages: *deepitalki,* a secret language no white man understands; and *talkitalki,* a concoction of many languages and idioms which I understood."

167. *Skulls plowed under.* Cf. Sharp, *The Last Aboriginal.*

168. *Griots:* "living encyclopedias." Giryama, Bantu, Amharic, Swahili, Yoruba, Vai, Thonga, Zulu, Jaba, Sudanese—these tribal scholars speak, with no basic change in idea and image, from line 173 to 214. The Africans have their *avant garde* in oral literature. Sometimes one of these bards becomes esoteric and sneers in a council of chiefs a line like this: "The snake walks on its belly." And thus elder statesmen are often puzzled by more than the seven ambiguities. Delafosse feared that the mass production technics introduced by missionaries and traders would contaminate art for art's sake in Africa.

170. These words of Guernier are no longer *ex cathedra:* the scope of a native culture is vertical—not horizontal.

194. *A stinkbug.* Cf. Kipling, *The White Man's Burden.*

221. Cf. Matthew VIII, xx.

226. V. *New York Times,* "Journey to Ararat," April 17, 1949. Cf. Maill's translation of a poem by an officer in the hospital at Erivan:

> "Here is Mount Ararat. It has a brooding look . . .
> One would think it was waiting to be set free."

230. *Uaz-Oîrit.* "The Very Green," the ancient Egyptian name for the Mediterranean.

239. *Netami lennowak*: "the first men."

240. Cf. Virgil, *Aeneid,* IV, 625: *"Exoriare aliquis!"*

245. *Prophet Jehudi Ashmun.* Lincoln University, the oldest Negro institution of its kind in the world, was founded as Ashmun Institute. The memory of the white pilgrim survives in old Ashmun Hall and in the Greek and Latin inscriptions cut in stones sacred to Lincoln men. The annual Lincoln-Liberian dinner is traditional, and two of the graduates have been ministers to Liberia.

249. V. Apollinaire, *La Chanson du Mal-Aimé,* the fifth and sixth sections.

258. *Miserere.* Cf. Newman, *The Definition of a Gentleman*: ". . . we attended the Tenebrae, at the Sestine, for the sake of the Miserere . . ."

262. *Cowled in azure*: the cloak of deceit and false humility. Cf. Hafiz, *The Divan* (*Odes*), V, translated by Bicknell.

264. *Whale and Elephant*: the symbols Jefferson used to designate Great Britain with her navy under Nelson and France with her army under Napoleon. V. Anderson, *Liberia,* X.

269. *Massebôth*: "sacred pillars." Cf. Genesis, XXVIII, xviii. Also the J author.

270. *Thou boy of tears.* Cf. Shakespeare, *Coriolanus,* V, v.

274. *Lachen mit vastchekes*: "laughing with needles being stuck in you"; ghetto laughter.

275. Cf. Blake, *The Tiger.*

276. Cf. Hardy, *The Convergence of the Twain.*

286. V. Pycraft, *Animals of the World,* 1941-1942. *A fortiori,* the American trotter is "a combination of barb and Arab on English stock."

287. V. Christy, *The Asian Legacy and American Life.* This book contains vital facts on Oriental influences in the New Poetry. What I owe the late Professor Arthur E. Christy, a favorite teacher, is not limited to the concept of "the shuttle ceaselessly weaving the warp and weft of the world's cultural fabric."

293. *Clochan-na-n'all*: "the blind men's stepping-stones." Cf. Ferguson, *The Welshmen of Tirawley.*

297. V. Aeschylus, *Agamemnon.*

301. Cf. Shakespeare, *Coriolanus*, I, i, 67-76. See also Mr. Traversi's essay on this phase of the play.

303. I came across these words somewhere: "The Ch'in emperor built the Great Wall to keep out Mongolian enemies from the north and burned the books of China to destroy intellectual enemies from within."

310. Cf. Akiba: "*Masôreth* is a fence for the sayings of the fathers."

312. *Adola mentis*. V. Bacon, *Novum Organum*.

313. *Divorcee Art*. Cf. Gourmont: "*Car je crois que l'art est par essence, absolument inintelligible au peuple.*"

325. *Pegasus' bomb*. Cf. Dobson, *On the Future of Poetry*.

326. V. Joshua VI, i.

327. Cf. Treitschke: "The State is Power. Of so unusual a type is its power, that it has no power to limit its power. Hence no treaty, when it becomes inconvenient, can be binding; hence the very notion of arbitration is absurd; hence war is a part of the Divine order." Contrast this idea with Lincoln's premise that the people can establish either a republic of wolves or a democracy of lambs, as instanced in the poem *The Dictionary of the Wolf*. Cf. Bismarck: "The clause *rebus sic stantis* is understood in all treaties."

330. *Curtain*. Cf. Crile, *A Mechanistic View of War and Peace, 1915*: "France [is] a nation of forty million with a deep-rooted grievance and an iron curtain at its frontier."

331. *Sancho's fears*. V. Cervantes, *Don Quixote de la Mancha*, Part II, translated by Peter Motteux, the episode of the letter: "To Don Sancho Pança, Governor of the Island of Barataria, to be delivered into his own hands, or those of his secretary."

332. *The Great Fear*. V. Madelin, *French Revolution*, 69.

333. Alberti, *Sobre los Angeles*.

334. Cf. the aphorism: "*La politique n'a pas d'entrailles.*"

335. Cf. Meredith, *Lucifer in Starlight*.

340. Cf. Hawthorne, *The Scarlet Letter*: "The black flower of civilized society, a prison."

344. V. Boccaccio, *The Three Rings*. Cf. Lessing, *Nathan the Wise*.

348. *Paseq*: "divider." This is a vertical line that occurs about 480 times in our Hebrew Bible. Although first mentioned in the *Midrash Rabba* in the eleventh century, it is still the most mysterious sign in the literature.

353. Cf. Cavafy, *Waiting for the Barbarians*.
354. *Famed enterprises*. V. Erasmus, *The Praise of Folly*, "Soldiers and Philosophers," *in toto*, the revised translation by John Wilson.
355. *Hearts of rags . . . souls of chalk*: Whitman's epithets for the "floating mass" that vote early and often for bread and circuses. *Hanorish tharah sharinas*: "Man is a being of varied, manifold, and inconstant nature." V. Della Mirandola, *Oration on the Dignity of Man*. Cf. Cunha: "The fantasy of universal suffrage [is] the Hercules' club of our dignity."
356. *Zinc buckets of verse*. V. Pasternak, *Definition of Poetry*. *Sugary grace*. Cf. Martial, *To a Rival Poet*.
359. Cf. Tennyson, *Idylls of the King*:
    "Red Ruin, and the breaking up of laws."
    V. Revelation VI. Cf. Jouve, *La Resurrection des Morts*. See the White Horse, the Red Horse, the Black Horse, and the fourth horse, the worst:
    "Tu es jaune et ta forme coule à ta charpente
    Sur le tonneau ajouré de tes côtes
    Les lambeaux verts tombent plus transparents
    La queue est chauve et le bassin a des béquilles
    Pour le stérile va-et-vient de la violence . . ."
363. *The Leveler*. V. The Acts V, xxxii-xxxvi.
367. *Pesiq*: "divided." V. Fuchs, *Pesiq ein Glossenzeichen*. It seems to me that this linguistic symbol gives us a concrete example of the teleological—perhaps the only one. By an accident of *a priori* probability, the sign in itself indicates both cause and effect, and the index of the relationship is served synchronously by either *paseq* or *pasiq*. Of course the protagonist of the poem uses them for his own purpose on another level.
369. *Bitter black estates*. Cf. Petrarca, *The Spring Returns, but Not to Him Returns*, translated by Auslander. *Buzzard*. V. Dryden, *The Hind and the Panther*. *Og*. V. Tate, *Second Part of Absalom and Achitophel*, the passage inserted by Dryden.
370. V. Rochester, *Satyr against Mankind*. Cf. Cocteau, *Le Cap de Bonne Espérance*: *"J'ai mal d'être homme."*
378. The watchword of Hidalgo, "Captain General of America."
380. Cf. Muselli, *Ballade de Contradiction*:
    "Fiers instants promis à la faux,
    Eclairs sombres au noir domaine!"

384. Cf. Camus, *The Artist as Witness of Freedom*: M. Desfourneau's ". . . demands were clear. He naturally wanted a bonus for each execution, which is customary in any enterprise. But, more important, he vigorously demanded that he be given . . . an administrative status. Thus came to an end, beneath the weight of history, one of the last of our liberal professions. . . . Almost everywhere else in the world, executioners have already been installed in ministerial chairs. They have merely substituted the rubber stamp for the axe."

386. Cf. Nietzsche, *Thus Spoke Zarathustra*, 232.

388. *Il Santo and Pero*: respectively, the nicknames of Nietzsche and Trotsky—the first innocently ironical, the second ironically innocent.

393. Cf. the remark of Nicholas I to a harassed minister of war: "We have plenty of little gray cattle." The Czar had in mind the Russian peasant.

397. *Brain-sick lands*. V. Meredith, *On the Danger of War*.

398. In the fable of Antisthenes, when the hares demanded equality for all, the lions said: "Where are your claws?" Cf. Martial, *Epigram XII*, 93: "*Dic mihi, si fias tu leo, qualis eris?*"

403. *Höhere*. Cf. Petronius: "*Proecipitandus est liber spiritus.*"

405. In the Gilded Era, cynics said of Babcock: "He fished for gold in every stinking cesspool." *Galerie des rois*. Cf. Verlaine, *Nocturne Parisien*, the reference to the twenty-eight statues of French kings.

406. *The seeking of cows*: this is the literal meaning of the word "battle" among the ancient Aryans who ravaged the Indo-Gangetic plains.The backwardness of their culture is attested by their failure to fumigate and euphemize their war aims. *Apartheid*: the South African system of multi-layered segregation.

410. *Deeds hostile all*: these words are from the *Chorus to Ajax*, by Sophocles, which Mr. Forrestal apparently read just before his death. *O Caton*: Cato the Younger committed suicide in 46 B. C. He had spent the previous night reading Plato's *Phaedo*. Cf. Lamartine, *Le Désespoir*.

411. *The walls*: "economic doctrines." The figure is Blok's.

414. *Sabotaged world*. Cf. Salmon, *Age de l'Humanité*.

415. V. Mitscherlich and Mielke, *Doctors of Infamy*, translated by Norden. Cf. Grotius, *De Jure Belli et Pacis*, "Prolegomena," XVIII: ". . . a people which violates the Laws of Nature and Nations, beats down the bulwark of its own tranquillity for future time."

417. Cf. Ronsard, *Le Bocage*. Also Musset, *La Nuit de mai*.

418. V. Gautier, *Vieux de la vieille*, the reference to Raffet's *nocturne* showing Napoleon's spirit reviewing spectral troops.

419. Plekhanov had Alexander II in mind when he used the trepan figure.

421. V. Cendrars, *Eloge de la vie dangereuse*.

422. Rimbaud, in a town near the Red Sea, looked toward Khartoum and wrote: *"Leur Gordon est un idiot, leur Wolseley un âne, et toutés leurs entreprises une suite insensée d'absurdités et de déprédations."* But fifty years later, when the Black Shirts entered Harrar, the ex-poet who plotted with Menelik against Italy was not there to hear Vittorio Mussolini's poetic account: "I still remember the effect produced on a small group of Galla tribesmen massed around a man in black clothes. I dropped an aerial bomb right in the center, and the group opened up like a flowering rose. It was most entertaining."

425. *Filets d'Arachné*. Cf. Chénier, *Qui? moi? de Phébus te dicter les leçons?*

426. *Mal éternel*. Cf. Lisle, *Dies irae*.

429. Cf. Baudelaire, *Le Voyage*.

430. V. Robinson, the Preface to *The Story of Medicine*.

431. *Yofan's studio*: Napoleon's old residence by the Kremlin wall. *Shkola Nenavisti*: a Berlin film on a Dublin subject in a Moscow theater.

432. *Otototoi*. See Gilbert Murray's Notes to *Aeschylus*.

433. Cf. Ovid, *Tristia*, quoted by Montaigne in *Of Three Commerces*. "Whoever of the Grecian fleet has escaped the Capharean rocks ever takes care to steer clear from those of the Euboean sea."

439. Cf. Lamartine: *"Il faut . . . Avec l'humanité t'unir par chaque pore."* Cf. Hugo, the Preface to *Les Contemplations*: "When I speak to you of myself, I am speaking to you of you." And again, Romains: *"Il faut bien qu'un jour on soit l'humanité!"*

454. *Black Aethiop.* Cf. Shakespeare, *Pericles*, II, ii:
       "A knight of Sparta, my renowned father,
       And the device he bears upon his shield
       Is a black Aethiop, reaching at the sun;
       The word, *'Lux tua vita mihi'*."
455. *Nullius in verba.* V. Lyons, *The Royal Society.*
464. *Grief-in-grain.* The "grain" I have in mind in this figure consists
       of the dried female bodies of a scale insect found on cacti in
       Mexico and Central America. The dye is red and unfading. Cf.
       Henley, *To James McNeill Whistler, in toto.*
479. Cf. Cavafy, *The Footsteps.*
480. *Gorii.* The voyage of the Carthaginian general Hanno carried
       him as far as what is now Liberia. The aborigines he saw were
       called *Gorii,* which later Greek and Latin scholars turned into
       "gorilla." However, to Hanno's interpreter and in the Wolof
       language today, the expression means "These too are men."
482. *Raya.* In the Turkish conquest of the Southern Slavs, the mal-
       treated people became *raya* or cattle. Conquest salves its con-
       science with contempt. Among the *raya* for five hundred years,
       the ballads of the wandering *guslars* kept freedom alive. *Oeil de
       Boeuf*: a waiting room at Versailles. Cf. Dobson, *On a Fan
       That Belonged to the Marquise de Pompadour.*
483. *Vsechelovek*: "universal man." In spite of its global image, this
       concept has a taint of *blut und boden.* Ever since Dostoevski,
       in a eulogy on Pushkin, identified the latter's genius with
       vsechelovek, the term has created pros and cons. Cf. the Latin:
       "Paul is a Roman and not a Roman." *Descamisados*: "the shirt-
       less ones."
484. The line was suggested by the history of the *Crudes* and *Asados*
       of Uruguay.
485. *Il Duce's Whore.* V. *Ciano Diaries 1939-43,* edited by Gibson.
       This is one of the "many instances of the vast contempt in
       which Il Duce held his people."
486. Cf. Milton, the outline of *Adam Unparadised.*
489. *Pelageya*: the wench of the Draft Constitution. V. Gogol, *Dead
       Souls. As seccas*: the devastating periodic droughts of Brazil.
491. *Taschunt.* Cf. Frobenius, *African Genesis,* 47 (Faber & Faber,
       Ltd.): "He felt that he had a thabuscht." A *mudwalled troy of
       jaguncos*: the home of Maciel's fanatics.
492. *Naze naze desu ka.* V. Mailer, *The Naked and the Dead,* the

diary of Major Ishimara, 247. Also Apollinaire, *Les Soupirs du Servant de Dakar*. *El grito de yara*: the watchword at Manzanillo, October 16, 1869.

494. Cf. Francia: ". . . now I know that bullets are the best saints you can have on the frontiers." *Bring out your dead*: the cry of the bellman walking by night in front of the deadcart. V. Defoe, *Journal of the Plague Year*.

495. *Aria*. Cf. Ludwig: "Dictatorship is always an aria, never an opera." *Sookin sin*. V. Duranty, *One Life, One Kopeck*, 3. *Breaks my shoulders*. Cf. Baudelaire: "*Pour ne pas sentir l'horrible fardeau du temps qui brise vos épaules et vous penche vers terre, il faut vous enivrer sans trêve.*"

496. *Lasciatemi morire*. V. Monteverdi, *Lament of Arianna*. Cf. Mendelssohn, *Aria from Elijah*: "O Lord, take away my life, for I am not better than my fathers." See also Mecaenas:

> "*Debilem, facito manu,*
> *Debilem pede, coxâ;*
> *Lubricos quate dentes:*
> *Vita dum superset, bene est . . .*"

Maneno matupu: "empty words," an epithet used in *deepitalki*—not *talki-talki*.

497. *Hog's Wash*: a London newspaper edited by Daniel Isaac Eaton during the "Anti-Jacobin Terror." Its name was an ironical allusion to Burke's epithet, "the swinish multitude."

498. *Savage's ten pounds*. Cf. Voltaire, *Irene*, the preliminary letter: "Shakespeare is a savage with sparks of genius in a dreadful darkness of night." See Shakespeare's will and epitaph.

500. *Here one singeth*. Cf. *Aucassin and Nocolete*, translated by Andrew Lang, the warning *aubade*, or "dawn song," of the sentinel on the tower above the trysting place.

502. When Croesus showed Solon his gold, the sage said: "Sir, if any other come that hath better iron than you, he will be master of all this gold."

504. *La légalité nous tue*. Muraviev, the Hangman, when he was governor-general of Poland, wrung this cry from the people.

507. *Vexilla regis prodeunt inferni*. Cf. Dante, *Inferno*, Canto XXXIV. *Tò tí*: "What is it?" This was the old gadfly's everlasting question.

508. Cf. Boileau, *Satires*, IV, 5-10.

509. *Tooth Puller*: "*Tiradentes*," the nickname of the first martyr of

Brazilian independence. *A cloaca of error.* See Pascal's doctrine of the Thinking Reed. Cf. Jarry, *Gestes et Opinions du Dr. Pataphysicien.*

510. *A belly's wolf.* Cf. Beaumont and Fletcher, *Woman Pleased.* Also Malley: "Religion is a process of turning your skull into a tabernacle, not of going up to Jerusalem once a year." *#13 with stars*: James Wilkinson, American general and secret Spanish agent, who sought to establish an empire in the Southwest under his own sword and sceptre.

511. Orlov in a letter to Golonin branded Muraviev as *"un homme de sac et de corde."*

512. *The Walk*: the *Peripatos* of the Lyceum.

513. *Epoch of the ant-hill.* V. Amiel, *Journal*: "The age of great men is going . . ."

514. *Shoulder-knots.* Cf. Swift, *A Tale of the Tub*, II.

515. *Dawn comes up like thunder.* Cf. Kipling, *Mandalay.*

516. *My pokazhem meeru*: "We'll show the whole world."

517. *The world is my parish*: Wesley's announcement of his mission.

518. *Hara ga hette iru*: "The belly has shrunken." *Higashi no kazeame*: the code words all Japanese embassies had received by mid-November, 1941. This phrase—"East wind rain"—was to be repeated in a short-wave news broadcast in case of a rupture in Japanese-American relations.

520. *O do de do de do de.* V. Shakespeare, *King Lear*, III, iv.

525. V. Newman, *The Dream of Gerontius.* Cf. Silva:

> *"Juan lanas, el mozo de esquina,*
> *Es absolutamente igual*
> *Al Emperador de la China;*
> *Los dos son un mismo animal."*

527. V. Luther:

> *"Ein feste Burg ist unser Gott*
> *Ein gute Wehr und Waffen."*

Voltaire looked upon the Seven Years' War as the devastation of Europe to settle whether England or France should win "a few acres of snow" in Canada.

528. *Satya bol gat hai*: "In truth lies salvation."

529. *Assalamu aleykum*: "Peace to you."

531. Cf. Napoleon's words to Czar Alexander at Tilsit, June 22, 1807: "If they want peace, nations should avoid the pin-pricks

that precede cannon-shots." *Mala' oun el yom yomek.* It is said
that Taha Shanin, the Dongolawi, as he plunged his spear into
General Gordon, cried: "O cursèd one, your time has come!"

532. *St. Innocent's.* Cf. Browne, *Hydriotaphia or Urn Burial.* Also
Job XIV, vii. The hag Today in the poem says the idiots have
a word for it. In China it means "Kong Hi Sing Yen"; in Africa,
"Happy Dashes"; in America, "Merry Christmas." Cf. F.P.A.,
For the Other 364 Days: "Christmas is over and Business is
Business."

533. *Brasses black and red.* Cf. Newbolt, *He Fell among Thieves.*
Also his *Clifton Chapel,* the inscription which gives an epitome
of two or three brasses in the Chapel:

> " 'Qui procul hinc,' the legend's writ—
> The frontier-grave is far away—
> 'Qui ante diem periit:
> Sed miles, sed pro patria'."

534. *Irritating parenthesis*: Cunha's figure for the problem of mis-
cegenation. V. Cunha, *Os Sertoes,* II, ii, 108-110.

537. *O sweet chariot*: I have in mind the Negro spiritual.

538. *Oh-mono*: "high-muck-a-mucks." *Greed's akeldama.* V. The
Acts I, xv-xxi.

541. *Demogorgon's mill.* Cf. Shelley, *Prometheus Unbound.*

546. *God in a rolls royce*: Father Divine. Some years ago in a jere-
miad issued from one of his "heavens" he announced that he
had reduced the Mayor of New York City "to a tittle of a jot"
during the Harlem riot.

547. *The seven trumpets.* Cf. Joshua VI, viii. *Today's baby boys*:
the code words for the A-bombs. The day after it was proved
at Alamagordo, New Mexico, that the weapon worked, the late
Henry L. Stimson, then secretary of war, received the message:
"Baby boy born today mother and child doing well."

548. In the days of the Norman King Stephen, men cried out that
"Christ and His saints slept."

549. *Dam-bid-dam*: "blood for blood." This was the way the Saadists
phrased the idea of talion at the Abbasiya mausoleum of No-
krashy Pasha. Cf. Leviticus XXIV, xvii-xxi.

551. *Souls of hyenas*: another reference to the bloody Muraview,
"this loathsome figure with a bulldog's face and a hyena's soul."
The phrase is from Kucharzewski. *Teneo te Africa*: the words

uttered by Caesar when he stumbled and fell on touching the shore of Africa. Cf. Suetonius, *Lives of the Caesars.*

552. *Mboagan:* "death."

554. *Rodinsmashedstatues.* The twisted version of the hag Today keeps her from seeing that only the hands of the statues have been chopped off; and thus she misses the apocalypse in the Rodin image, the magnetic needle of whose compass pivots toward the Africa-To-Be (*Höhere* and *Khopirû*), set as the goal, by the protagonist, in the first section. For an elucidation of this transitional Janus-faced image, see Lajos Egri, *The Art of Dramatic Writing,* 30-31. *Aleppe.* Cf. Dante, *Inferno,* Canto VII: "*Pape Satan! pape, aleppe!*"

555. *Tomorrow.* V. Blake, *The Bard.* Cf. Rimbaud: "*Je vais dévoiler tous les mystères . . . mort, naissance, avenir, passé, cosmogonie, néant.*" Also Goethe, *Faust,* 7433:

"Enough, the poet is not bound by time."

558. *The fatal verse.* Alexander the Great made Black Clitus, "his best beloved," King of Bactria and commander of his celebrated cavalry, which synchronized with the Macedonian phalanx to deliver a battle's one-two punch. Dropsica, Clitus' mother, was Alexander's nurse. During the Persian campaign, a furious argument broke out at the king's supper table. He snatched a spear from a soldier and ran it through Clitus as he came from behind a curtain shouting a verse from Euripides' *Andromache:*

"In Greece, alas, how ill things ordered are!"

V. Plutarch, *Lives,* "Alexander." Cf. Shakespeare, *Hamlet,* III, iv.

559. The epithet African intellectuals give to Johánnesburg.

560. The German army's nickname for General Dumas, who rescued Napoleon from the Mamelukes by riding a stallion into a mosque in Cairo. The general's astounding feats kept him from getting a marshal's baton. He never recovered from the blow.

561. Cf. Xenophanes: "Men have always made their gods in their own images—the Greeks like Greeks, the Ethiopians like Ethiopians." Again Professor Christy's figure of "the world's cultural fabric" is evidenced in the statues of the Black Virgin Mary and Negro saints which were common in Germany and Latin Europe, as well as northern Africa, during the Middle Ages. The stained glass of the Cathedral at Chartres has portraits in

ebony. *Creation's Hell Hole*: the name the Italians gave the Danakil Desert.

566. Cf. Moog, *Um Rio imita o Rheno*. Moog created his symbol to suggest the heavy German settlement in Rio Grande do Sul. The line indicates a historical parallel when 10,000 Negroes gathered in Lisbon and threatened to outnumber the whites.

567. *Kitab al sudan wa'lbidan*: "the superiority of the black race over the white." Before the swastika gave Nordicism the Stuka, an Arab scholar, Al-Jahiz, issued his racist theory in reverse: another instance of similarity in dissimilarity.

570. *Pehleh*: "money." *Nash Barin*: before the October Revolution, this expression meant "Our Master" or God. I don't know its present meaning. Cf. I Timothy VI, v. Also Milton, *Paradise Lost*, 678.

573. *The chattel*: "Tariq." *Rock*: Gibraltar was named for this black general and ex-slave. *The Rime of the upstart Crow*. Cf. Shakespeare, *Sonnet* LV:
> "Not marble, nor the gilded monuments
> Of princes, shall outlive this powerful rime."

574. *Ppt. knows*. V. Swift, *Journal to Stella*, March 15, 1712.

577. *Parsifal-Feirefiz*. Cf. Eschenbach, *Parsifal*. Also Du Bois, *The World and Africa*, X.

580. *Cest prace*: "all honor to labor."

587. *70A subway*. V. Wilson, *Liberia*, for many of these references.

590. The Zorzor twins were miracle-workers in iron, see line 273.

610. *Khopirû*: "To Be." The concept embraces the Eternity of Thence, which, free from blind necessity, contains the good life.

619. *Shikata-gai-nai*: "It cannot be helped." This is the stoicism with which Japanese villagers meet the earth convulsions of sacred Fujiyama. In other lands it is fate, kismet, predestination, artistries of Circumstance, economic determinism, necessitarianism—from Aeschylus' Nemesis to Chénier's *filets d'Arachné*. Sometimes it takes the form of the sophistry, *human nature does not change*. As a hidden premise it blocks the kinetic; it confuses the feral with the societal and leads to *petitio principii*. History, then, remains a Heraclitean continuum of a world flaring up and dying down as "it always was, is, and shall be." Some moderns have turned this ancient seesaw figure of a crude

dialectics into a locomotive of history. In the poem, however, the flux of men and things is set forth in symbols whose motions are vertical-circular, horizontal-circular, and rectilinear. In spite of the diversity of phenomena, the underlying unity of the past is represented by the ferris wheel; the present by the merry-go-round; and the future by the automobile, the train, the ship, and the aeroplane. I placed the ship image in the middle of the images of swifter vehicles to indicate the contradiction in the essence of things, the struggle of opposites, which mankind will face even in *Khopirû* and *Höhere*. By the Law of Relativity, history will always have its silver age as well as its golden, and each age will contain some of the other's metal. Because of these upward and onward lags and leaps, it is not an accident that Liberia reaches her destination, the Parliament of African Peoples, after the aerial symbol. Cf. Meredith, *The World's Advance*, the figure of the reeling spiral.

620. *Ars of Phidias.* Cf. Rodin: "Beyond Phidias sculpture will never advance." Also Shakespeare, *Troilus and Cressida*:
> "The baby figure of the giant mass
> Of things to come.

627. *Nidaba.* Cf. Dr. Samuel Noah Kramer's translation of a Sumerian tablet in the Museum of the Ancient Orient: "You have exalted Nidaba, the queen of the places of learning."

680. *Le Premier des Noirs.* When Napoleon became First Consul, Toussaint L'Ouverture addressed him in this manner: "From the First of the Blacks to the First of the Whites."

691-692. *The Very Black:"Qim-Oîrit,"* or the Red Sea. V. Maspero, *The Dawn of Civilization,* I.

699-700. Cf. Beethoven, *Ninth Symphony,* "Finale."

702-703. *Heralds of earth and water:* ancient symbols of submission.

707. In this phrase Hugo was describing Hugo.

727. *Siyáfa:* "We Die."

728-729. *Geh Tai Gea:* "All Is Well."

734. *The Violent Men:* the stigmatized advocates of the Declaration of Independence in the First and Second Continental Congresses. V. Meigs, *The Violent Men.*

737. *Afrika sikelél' iAfrika:* "Africa save Africa."